Emergency Vehicles

Fire Trucks

Chris Oxlade

QEB Publishing

Published in the United States by
QEB Publishing, Inc.
3 Wrigley, Suite A
Irvine, CA 92618

www.qeb-publishing.com

Library of Congress Cataloging-in-Publication Data

Oxlade, Chris.
Fire truck / Chris Oxlade.
p. cm. -- (QEB emergency vehicles)
Includes index.
ISBN 978-1-59566-978-0 (hardcover)
1. Fire engines--Juvenile literature. I. Title.
TH9372.O976 2010
628.9'259--dc22

2009005878

ISBN 978-1-59566-689-5 (paperback)

Printed and bound in the United States of America in North Mankato, Minnesota

092809
QED 10-2009 7

Author Chris Oxlade
Editor Eve Marleau
Designer Susi Martin

Publisher Steve Evans
Creative Director Zeta Davies
Managing Editor Amanda Askew

Picture credits
(t=top, b=bottom, l=left, r=right, c=center, fc=front cover)
Alamy
5t Firephoto; 7r Blue shadows; 9r Blue shadows; 11 Jack Sullivan;
16r EuroStyle Graphics; 19r Michael Routh
Corbis
12–13 Patrick Bennett; 15 Transtock
Photolibrary
8–9 Charles Schuck
Pierce Manufacturing, Inc., an Oshkosh Corporation company
4-5; 6-7
Shutterstock
Tyler Olsen; 10b Christoffer Vika; 13t Monkey Business Images; 14 Mike Brake; 17–18 Christoffer Vika; 18–19 Ivan Cholakov; 20–21 Gaby Kooijman; 21r Slavko Sereda

Words in **bold** can be found in the glossary on page 23.

Contents

What is a fire truck?

A fire truck is an **emergency** vehicle. Fire trucks help **firefighters** to put out fires. They also help with other emergencies, such as rescues and floods.

In the United States, some cities use aerial trucks. They have a special long ladder.

Firefighters wear fireproof suits, helmets, and strong boots to protect them from the heat of the flames.

Firefighters also pump away floodwater using the hoses.

Parts of a fire truck

There are many different types of fire trucks. Most trucks are called **pumpers** or tenders. They are used in many different rescues.

This fire truck has a large water tank inside, a water **pump**, **hoses**, ladders, and other special equipment.

Ladder

NORTH CANTON

Lockers

Ladders can be used to rescue people from windows in burning buildings.

Pumps and hoses

Fire trucks have an on-board water pump. The fire truck's engine makes the pump work.

A pump can suck up 1,000 gallons (4,000 liters) of water into the hoses every minute—that's enough to fill 30 bathtubs!

A fire truck carries many hoses. There are hoses to bring water to the truck's pump and hoses to carry water to the fire.

Firefighters get water from fire hydrants.

Fire truck equipment

Fire trucks carry a lot of equipment that firefighters need to rescue people. There are metal cutters, **portable** water pumps, digging tools, and **breathing masks**.

This firefighter is using a metal cutter.

The equipment is kept in lockers along the sides of the truck. Firefighters check this equipment every day to make sure it's safe to use.

Emergency!

Fire trucks and firefighters are always ready for action. When an emergency call comes, the firefighters jump right into their trucks.

Flashing lights and noisy **sirens** on the fire truck warn people to move out of the way and let the truck through.

As they drive to a fire, firefighters put on their fireproof clothes and prepare for action.

Ladder trucks

A ladder truck is a fire truck with a long ladder on its back. Firefighters climb up the ladder to rescue people from windows and to spray water.

The ladder is then lowered when the truck is not being used.

The ladder is **telescopic**. This means that sections of the ladder slide out to make it longer.

Airport fire trucks

Airports have their own special fire trucks. The trucks are always ready in case a fire starts on a plane during takeoff or landing.

Foam is made by mixing detergent, or soap, with water.

On top of an airport fire truck is a hose called a monitor. It sprays foam over a fire. The foam covers the flames and puts them out.

Cross-country trucks

Forest fires can be difficult to put out. The ground can be rough, and the fire spreads quickly. Firefighters use special trucks with on-board water tanks to fight forest fires.

This fire truck has a metal cage to protect its crew from falling branches.

Forest firefighters also use **four-wheel-drive** pickup trucks. They carry water and equipment to put out small fires.

It can be easier to reach a forest fire in a four-wheel-drive truck.

In air and on water

Firefighters also work in the air and on the water. Firefighting boats spray water onto fires in buildings along river banks. They also help to fight fires on ships at sea.

Firefighting aircraft are often used to fight forest fires. Helicopters and **fixed-wing aircraft** drop water onto the flames from above.

Firefighting aircraft scoop up water from rivers or lakes and drop it onto the flames.

Port of Rotterdam

Port Authority

Activities

- Which picture shows an airport truck, a ladder truck, and a firefighting plane?

- Make a drawing of your favorite fire truck. What kind of truck is it? Does it have lights and sirens? What color is it?
- Write a story about a fire. It could be anywhere in the world—or even on another planet! What truck would you drive? How big would the fire be? How dangerous would it be? How long would it take to put it out?
- Which of these fire trucks would be used to put out a fire at sea?

Glossary

Breathing mask
A mask that lets a firefighter breathe in a smoke-filled building.

Emergency
A dangerous situation that must be dealt with right away.

Firefighter
A person whose job it is to fight fires.

Fixed-wing aircraft
An aircraft with two wings that are fixed to its body.

Foam
A frothy material made from water filled with soapy bubbles.

Four-wheel-drive vehicle
A vehicle with four wheels that are all turned by its engine.

Hose
A long tube through which water flows.

Portable
Something that can be carried around.

Pump
A machine that sucks in and pushes water along hoses.

Pumper
A fire truck that is used in many emergency situations.

Siren
A machine that makes a loud noise.

Telescopic
When parts slide over each other to make something such as a ladder longer or shorter.

Index